Unto Us

A Christmas Poetry Book

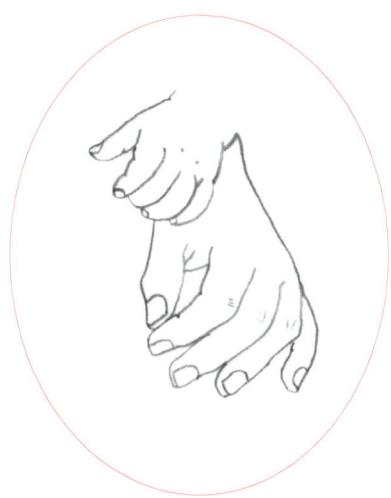

Lisa Belknap

Veery Glade Publishing

Unto Us: A Christmas Poetry Book
Copyright © 2018 by Lisa Belknap
Illustrations by Lisa Belknap
Cover Design by Roseanna White

All scriptures quotations are taken from
the Holy Bible, KING JAMES VERSION (KJV):
KING JAMES VERSION, public domain.

All rights reserved. No part of this book may be used, stored, or reproduced in any manner: electronic, mechanical, photocopying, recording, or otherwise, without written permission from the author. A short quotation of a few lines used for private non-commercial individual or in printed reviews is fully encouraged and no written permission is needed in such cases.

Little Baby King was previously published in the 2015 Christmas issue of the *War Cry* magazine.

ISBN-13:978-1-7327930-0-2

Veery Glade Publishing
Cortland, New York 13045

*In Honor and Memory
of my Family*

Contents

In His Image **7**
A Lasting Covenant **9**
An Amazing Birth **11**
Baby in a Basket **12**
My Kinsman Redeemer **15**
The Player of the Harp **16**
Unto Us **19**
In That Day **21**
The Zeal of the LORD **22**
Christmas Faith **24**
Who Would Love, Obey, and Carry **27**
Leap for Joy **28**
Prepare the Way **30**
Mary **32**
Jesus, Name above All Names **35**
A Savior Has Been Born to You **37**
Little Baby King **39**
Good Shepherds Say **40**
The Bethlehem Star **43**
The Birth of Hope **44**
Our Heart Revealed **47**
Cry of Redemption **48**
Red Is for Atonement **51**
Unto Me **53**
Christmas Love **55**

**So God created man in his *own* image,
in the image of God created he him;
male and female created he them.
Genesis 1:27**

In His Image

Who is God like and what is His image?
Which features form His human visage?
They were the first, a rose to breathe—
the start of love with Adam and Eve.

Where did God walk in the Garden of Eden?
Why would He care for men and women?
They were the first, no loss to grieve—
friendship began with Adam and Eve.

How would God give a tender spirit?
When would a baby sweetly mirror it?
They were the first, to have, receive—
the face of God on Adam and Eve.

**AFTER these things
the word of the LORD
came unto Abram in a vision, saying,
Fear not, Abram: I *am* thy shield,
and thy exceeding great reward.
Genesis 15:1**

A Lasting Covenant

Looking across the breadth of time,
the loving Master Planner
promised us a great reward
beneath earth's starry banner.

On faithful souls like Abraham,
who counted stars at night,
a righteousness is credited.
Be one who sees the Light!

Vows made by God alone endure.
He chose a timeless mercy.
His Word will always come to pass.
Return is never empty.

Eternal reward, a trusted shield,
the Father sends the Lamb.
For us, a lasting covenant
comes from the great "I AM."

**And Sarah said,
God hath made me to laugh,
so that all that hear will laugh with me.
Genesis 21:6**

An Amazing Birth

Now here is Sarah, very, very old Sarah,
who once was a pretty, young girl,
who once was a woman very beautiful,
a priceless, shining pearl.

No longer a princess, she's ninety years old,
with bones and joints failing fast.
Her child-bearing years many years ago—
they ended, they're gone, they're past!

Is there a challenge for Almighty God?
What is too difficult for doing?
Can He not do as He says He will—
creating, restoring, renewing?

Sarah had a baby at a very old age,
and with her delight we laugh!
For nothing is impossible with the LORD
who works on our behalf.

Baby in a Basket

The power of the LORD: Magnificent! Behold!
Tremendous signs and wonders continue to unfold.

Moses, the humblest, stood on Nebo's stand,
and talked with our Father near the promised land.

He gave the written Law, the message that condemns,
to show the cost of freedom the Holy Spirit hems.

The Lamb of God will save. Atonement was explained.
And faith in God's provision upon the earth maintained.

Like Noah and his family surviving the flood,
God again delivered when doors were marked in blood.

With Moses, I sing too— "From slavery, I am free!
The horse and its rider are thrown into the sea."

And there was Jochebed, avoiding any casket.
She placed upon the river her baby in a basket.

**For if the ministration
of condemnation *be* glory,
much more doth the ministration
of righteousness exceed in glory.
2 Corinthians 3:9**

**And he said, Who *art* thou?
And she answered I *am* Ruth
thine handmaid: spread therefore
thy skirt over thine handmaid;
for thou *art* a near kinsman.
Ruth 3:9**

My Kinsman Redeemer

Guide me, Lord, through all my days,
I choose to follow You.
I come from a distant land afar
to place my trust in You.

Spread over me Your garment fair
and take me as Your own,
and hide me in Your loving care,
until I reach my home.

By Your wounds, I have been healed.
You took away my blame.
Your precious blood has purchased me
and transferred every shame.

Jesus is my Kinsman Redeemer—
my voice will brightly sing.
From Christmas to forever,
a daughter of the King.

The Player of the Harp

The player of the harp plays on,
in the fields of Bethlehem,
increasing skill and aptitude,
while flocks he would attend.

His touch upon the strings will tell
of a heart to one day rule,
of a man after the LORD's own heart,
of a worth o'er any jewel.

He will sing, "The LORD stands before me now,"
when he strikes the harp to ring.
"Surely love and goodness follow me,"
as he makes the lyre sing.

"God is my Rock," David fills the air,
melodies heard near and far.
And tones echo over the distant fields
of the coming Morning Star.

**I Jesus have sent mine angel
to testify unto you these things
in the churches. I am the root
and the offspring of David,**
and **the bright and morning star.
Revelation 22:16**

**For unto us a child is born,
unto us a son is given:
and the government shall be upon his shoulder:
and his name shall be called Wonderful,
Counsellor, The mighty God,
The everlasting Father,
The Prince of Peace.
Isaiah 9:6**

Unto Us

Isaiah spoke the call
of a Great Light shone for all;
the long-awaited prophecy
of a precious baby sent for me.

And I know
that the snow
is as white,
that the light
is as clear,
that the tear
is as wet,
that the debt
is as gone,
that the dawn
is as bold
as was foretold!

And I think of the baby
and I marvel and I wonder.
Yes, I kneel on my knees,
and I wonder.

**But thou, Bethlehem Ephratah, *though* thou be little among the thousands of Judah, *yet* out of thee shall he come forth unto me *that is* to be ruler in Israel; whose goings forth *have been* from of old, from everlasting.
Micah 5:2**

In That Day

Now here is Micah, a citizen of Judah,
declaring there will be trouble.
The LORD will destroy what the people have done.
There shall be piles of rubble!

Disaster will strike and gone be the trust.
The LORD shall hide His face.
The mire in the streets will become as dust
blown away, without a trace!

Yet, in *that* day sounds the joy of triumph.
A remnant will live in peace.
Kingship shall reign from Jerusalem—
restoration, full and complete!

And our sins sink down in the pit of earth—
He will hurl them into the sea—
stemming from our faith in Bethlehem's birth
and the payment at Calvary!

The *Zeal* of the LORD

The zeal of the LORD is mighty.
Who can see, who can hear, who can know
how He forms distant starry byways,
how He measures depths of snow?

How, you say, can the LORD be loving,
passionate for each of us?
How can rainbows flare a dark sky?
How a Star draw close to us?

God is Love. His very nature—
by His Word, it comes to be,
like the earth and moon and rivers,
like the mountains and the sea.

For the LORD's renown, it is
in an instant pregnancy.
His life for eternal life,
and the joy of the redeemed.

**And the angel answered and said unto her,
The Holy Ghost shall come upon thee,
and the power of the Highest
shall overshadow thee:
therefore also that holy thing
which shall be born of thee
shall be called
the Son of God.
Luke 1:35**

Christmas Faith

I believe in God
giving Christmas cheer—
the love, the peace, the songs,
my heart in faith belongs
to children drawing near.

I believe in Christ
holding Christmas love—
the joy, the hope, the light,
faces turning bright
with promise from above.

I believe the Ghost,
sealing Christmas whole—
His truth, His word, His keeping,
angels watch our sleeping,
and blessings for my soul.

**And blessed *is* she that believed:
for there shall be a performance
of those things which were told her
from the Lord.
Luke 1:45**

**Then Joseph being raised from sleep
did as the angel of the Lord had bidden him,
and took unto him his wife.
Matthew 1:24**

Who Would Love, Obey, and Carry

Who would love, obey and carry,
and not linger, and not tarry,
see an angel, fierce and scary,
and become a visionary,
knowing wonders many, very,
in the Father's sanctuary,
having faith necessary,
and a duty customary,
with joy extraordinary,
from a heart, good and merry,
but the man who would marry
Mary.

Leap for Joy

Leap for joy! Hear the highest greeting.
By the Spirit, wonders in the meeting.
Sing of love! See, the Lord's preparing.
Saving grace! Miracles declaring.

Elizabeth knew, as her heart was willing,
to let come in the Holy Spirit's filling.
Zechariah, too, with trust and naming,
spread the joy with songs proclaiming.

Leap for joy! Christmas time for sharing.
By the Spirit, grateful hearts for caring.
Sing of love! Carols all for bringing.
Saving grace! Christmas bells are ringing.

**For, lo, as soon as the voice
of thy salutation sounded
in mine ears, the babe leaped
in my womb for joy.
Luke 1:44**

Prepare the Way

Prepare the way to the path of peace,
on which Christ's joy will never cease,
and of whose government's increase
will never end.

Prepare the way to forgiveness sweet
from nail-pierced hands and nail-pierced feet
of Him, who, blood upon the seat,
became our friend.

Prepare the way to redemption sure,
the Great Physician, meek and pure,
bore the sins of the world and for
our wounds to mend.

Prepare the way to the victory won,
repent and baptize in the Son,
who will, the risen, conquering one,
our souls attend.

**And thou, child, shalt be called
the prophet of the Highest: for thou shalt go
before the face of the Lord
to prepare his ways.
Luke 1:76**

Mary

Merciful, tender, kind, and true—
God must have seen a goodness in you.
For you were the one
who cradled the sun
and rocked in the billowy blue.

Admirable, seeker, wise, and smart—
God must have known a little girl's heart.
For you saw the light
that shone in the night
and bowed to a low, humbling part.

Radical, servant, strong, and just—
God must have loved a young woman's trust.
For you caught the breeze
that came through the trees
and spun in a heavenly gust.

Yearning-full, giver, gentle dove—
God must have held a mother of love.
For you kissed the face
of redeeming grace
and loved who was yours from above.

**And the angel said unto her,
Fear not, Mary: for thou hast found
favour with God. And, behold,
thou shalt conceive in thy womb,
and bring forth a son,
and shalt call his name JESUS.
Luke 1:30-31**

**Wherefore God also hath
highly exalted him, and given him
a name which is above every name.
Philippians 2:9**

Jesus, Name above All Names

Jesus, name above all names;
The LORD Saves from fiery flames.
Messiah, Christ, Lamb of God;
Merry Christmas to you all!

El Elohim, El Shaddai;
Ancient of Days, hear our cry.
Emmanuel, Anointed One;
Merry Christmas to you all!

Son of God, Chief Cornerstone;
Man of Sorrows to atone.
The King of Kings, Good Shepherd;
Merry Christmas to you all!

Unspeakable Gift, Star Out of Jacob;
Wonderful Counselor fills us up.
The Rock, the Lily, Prince of Peace;
Merry Christmas to you all!

Savior, Dayspring, Rose of Sharon;
Jesus— name over everyone.
Light of the World, Risen Son;
Merry Christmas to you all!

**For unto you is born this day
in the city of David a Saviour,
which is Christ the Lord.
And this *shall be* a sign unto you;
Ye shall find the babe wrapped
in swaddling clothes,
lying in a manger.
Luke 2:11-12**

A Savior Has Been Born to You

Who can create distant worlds
and give the sky its hue?
I think of the words the angel spoke,
"A Savior has been born to you."

Who can stop earth and blazing fire
and allow a donkey to talk,
and an eagle to yell the final woe—
on water, the faithful walk?

It's God, Creator of human life.
He married our characteristics.
His Word became flesh in Mary's arms.
How merry, marry-full, mystic!

His radiance is Jesus Christ,
the Son— Faithful and True.
And saved, I hear the proclaiming words,
"A Savior has been born to you."

**I will declare the decree:　　　
The LORD hath said unto me,　　
Thou *art* my Son;　　　　　
This day have I begotten thee.　
Psalm 2:7**

Little Baby King

Little finger, little toe,
He controls the wind and snow!
By His hand, He whips the tow
down beneath the ocean low.

Little laugh, little coo,
He can make the old brand new!
At His voice, for me and you,
He has ripped the veil in two.

Button nose, twinkling eyes,
He will raise the one who dies!
Through His eyes, we realize
what is truth and what are lies.

Baby Jesus, King of Kings,
Precious are the little things!
Oh, to own the heart that sings
of the joy salvation brings!

Good Shepherds Say

The angel spoke, good shepherds woke,
and they were terrified.
From Heaven's throne a glory shone.
"The Lord be glorified!"

"Good news is here, the Babe is near,"
great voices multiplied,
with praise aloud from Heaven's cloud.
"The Son be glorified!"

The shepherds ran, the news began,
the streets they occupied.
The people heard the joyous word.
"The King be glorified!"

And to this day, good shepherds say,
"Let love be magnified."
Our hearts in song to Him belong.
"May Christ be glorified!"

**And when they had seen *it*,
they made known abroad
the saying which was told them
concerning this child.
Luke 2:17**

**NOW when Jesus was born
in Bethlehem of Judea in the days
of Herod the king, behold, there came
wise men from the east to Jerusalem,
Saying, Where is he that is born
King of the Jews? for we have seen
his star in the east, and are come
to worship him.
Matthew 2:1-2**

The Bethlehem Star

Joyfully twinkling, high up above,
proclaiming news of God's great love.
And there I see it glimmer afar,
the wonder of the Bethlehem Star!

Eternal brightness, vivid and clear,
without an equal, without a peer.
And there I shake on the path at night,
as we enter in majestic light.

Shimmering goodness, warmth all around,
bathing the Christ Child and all who abound.
And there I kneel with my gift of myrrh,
believing well and calmly sure.

Unsurpassed beauty, a gem in the sky,
an emblem of change, a beacon at nigh.
And there I bow near the Baby King
and marvel as the angels sing.

Splendidly brilliant, a stately sign,
glistening truth, a radiant shine.
And there I trust, heading home afar,
the glory of the Bethlehem Star.

The Birth of Hope

Shall I compare hope to a baby's smile?
Hope is more vibrant and more permanent.
Sweet smiles may soothe a mother for a while,
and babies often change with malcontent.

Sometimes, low cries go down to nethergloom,
where weeping, mourning, loss and darkness grow,
as when the babes of Bethlehem faced doom,
and Rachel wept through days of utter woe.

But hope, which gives a peace and trust anew,
smiles brighter in the Master Spirit's plan.
The knowing longings are fulfilled is true.
Eternal life is birthed in God's own man.

That man, who was a babe, is Jesus Christ.
The birth of hope begins with Jesus Christ.

**Thus saith the LORD; Refrain thy voice from weeping, and thine eyes from tears: for thy work shall be rewarded, saith the LORD; and they shall come again from the land of the enemy. And there is hope in thine end, saith the LORD, that thy children shall come again to their own border.
Jeremiah 31:16-17**

**Then took he him up in his arms,
and blessed God, and said, Lord,
now lettest thou thy servant depart
in peace, according to thy word:
For mine eyes have seen thy salvation.
Luke 2:28-30**

Our Heart Revealed

The broken healed.
The promise sealed.
Simeon knew the baby, too.

Through darkest night
shines saving light.
By love's intent, salvation sent.

In heart and soul,
completion, whole.
Sure be the days of Heaven's ways.

This cradled heart
will soon impart
our sin repealed, our heart revealed.

Cry of Redemption

Now here is Anna from Asher,
a prophetess, old and wise,
who cried out for years, "Redemption!"
then saw it with her own eyes.

Who learns of freedom, but those
who've been in captivity?
Who longs for restoration,
but ones who are incomplete?

Who gains forgiveness, but them
that repent of their sin?
Who reaps a full recovery,
but people who cry to Him?

With Anna, give thanks to God
for the cry of redemption is here,
in the baby King named Jesus
and the Kingdom of God near.

**And she coming in that instant
gave thanks likewise unto the Lord,
and spake of him to all them that looked
for redemption in Jerusalem.
Luke 2:38**

**For this is my blood
of the new testament,
which is shed for many
for the remission of sins.
Matthew 26:28**

Red Is for Atonement

The reddest, purest, deepest blood
from royalty divine
is the only begotten Son of God.
My heart has made Him mine.

The richest blood for me He shed;
the highest cost was spent.
Accomplishment by Him who bled—
red is for atonement.

Now, look to skies of deepest red
in dawn's sure rapture morning.
The day will be as Heaven said—
joy replacing mourning.

On we wait, as skies go by,
for waking in the fields
of roses, reddest to our eye,
and smells the new land yields.

**For God so loved the world,
that he gave his only begotten Son,
that whosoever believeth in him
should not perish,
but have everlasting life.
John 3:16**

Unto Me

There are two roads a traveler can go.
Far long ago, I chose my way.
My mother knelt beside me low.
In heart, I knew my joy would grow
forever, day by day.

My childhood faith made me see,
kneeling there beside the bed,
that God loves me for eternity.
He sent His Son to die for me.
On the cruel cross, He bled.

By asking Him to enter in,
within my little frame,
the Holy Spirit would then begin
to guide me, like a wind within.
I'd never be the same.

I chose the road of Life. With zeal,
I'll be telling this ages hence—
how He saved me with a perfect seal,
from my believing He is real,
and that has made all the difference.

**And the King shall answer and say
unto them, Verily I say unto you,
Inasmuch as ye have done *it* unto one
of the least of these my brethren,
ye have done *it* unto me.
Matthew 25:40**

Christmas Love

Love is patient, love is kind.
God became His human kind.
Have you held the highest gifting?
Do you know your bondage lifting?

On your way, and to others,
have you helped sisters, brothers?
Have you fed and attended?
Have you clothed and amended?

Visits too, in prisons dark,
have you prayed in places stark?
Did you ask the stranger in?
Did you tend the sick within?

Eternal reward, a trusted shield—
to love and care will greatly yield.
The face of Jesus on my pilgrimage—
Christmas love, in His image.

Additional Bible Verses to Cherish

Behold, I *am* the LORD, the God of all flesh: is there any thing too hard for me? **Jeremiah 32:27**

So shall my word be that goeth forth out of my mouth: it shall not return unto me void, but it shall accomplish that which I please, and it shall prosper *in the thing* whereto I sent it. **Isaiah 55:11**

And the Word was made flesh, and dwelt among us, (and we beheld his glory, the glory as of the only begotten of the Father,) full of grace and truth. **John 1:14**

Who is the image of the invisible God, the firstborn of every creature. **Colossians 1:15**

But God commendeth his love toward us, in that, while we were yet sinners, Christ died for us. **Romans 5:8**

And said unto them, Thus it is written, and thus it behoved Christ to suffer, and to rise from the dead the third day: And that repentance and remission of sins should be preached in his name among all nations, beginning at Jerusalem. **Luke 24:46-47**

Whosoever shall confess that Jesus is the Son of God, God dwelleth in him, and he in God. **1 John 4:15**

And Simeon blessed them, and said unto Mary his mother, Behold, this child is set for the fall and rising again of many in Israel; and for a sign which shall be spoken against; (Yea, a sword shall pierce through thy own soul also,) that the thoughts of many hearts may be revealed. **Luke 2:34-35**

For the Father judgeth no man, but hath committed all judgment unto the Son. **John 5:22**

Cast not away therefore your confidence, which hath great recompence of reward. **Hebrews 10:35**

Acknowledgements

I am thankful to our Heavenly Father for His provision of:

…friends. Thank you Cheryl Elton, Sarah Lynn Phillips,
Bonnie Swinehart, Vie Stallings Herlocker, Kate Hodges,
Mary Elsasser, Beth Westcott, Karen Dove, Cheryl Farnholtz,
Julie Ryan, DeeDee Tongue, Brenda O'Gorman,
Cathy Lee, and Diana Curatolo.

…prayer warrior friends.

…family. Thank you to my daughter, Malin,
and son, Ezra, for assistance on the computer,
to my loving and faithful parents,
and other faithful relatives who have gone on before me.
And to Matthew, my husband, who endured with me.

…and you, the reader, for taking time to meditate
on the true meaning of Christmas.
May your heart keep the awesome light of truth from
God's love unto us through His Son,
Jesus Christ, our Lord and Savior.

Other books include:
Seasons of Love: Woodland Poems of God's Love
and
The Long Skip Home (Middle Grade Fantasy).

Visit me at poemsandprayer.blogspot.com.

www.ingramcontent.com/pod-product-compliance
Lightning Source LLC
LaVergne TN
LVHW010035070426
835507LV00006B/143